OCT - - 2014

THE BASICS OF
MECHANICS

THE BASICS OF MECHANICS

JOHN O. E. CLARK

Rosen
PUBLISHING®

New York

This edition published in 2015 by:

The Rosen Publishing Group, Inc.
29 East 21st Street
New York, NY 10010

Library of Congress Cataloging-in-Publication Data

Clark, John O. E.
The basics of mechanics/by John O. E. Clark.
    p. cm.—(Core concepts)
Includes bibliographic references and index.
ISBN 978-1-4777-7754-1 (library binding)
1. Mechanics—Juvenile literature. 2. Matter—Properties—Juvenile literature. I. Clark, John Owen Edward. II. Title.
QC127.4 C54 2015
531—d23

Manufactured in the United States of America

© 2004 Brown Bear Books Ltd.

CONTENTS

CHAPTER ONE

UNDERSTANDING MEASUREMENTS

Measurement is at the heart of physics. Indeed, observation and measurement are central to the whole of science. Measurement requires units to express how heavy, how long, or how old something is. Science uses a wide range of units that measure everything from the size of an atom to the age of the universe.

In everyday life we use a variety of units, usually chosen to suit the thing that we are measuring. For instance, we measure the distance to the next town or city in miles, the size of a parking lot in yards, the height of a flagpole in feet, and the size of a piece of paper in inches. These are all units of length—distance is simply a length along the ground, and a height is a length measured in an upward direction.

But such a mixture of units can be a nuisance, as we find out when we have to do the math involved in changing inches to feet or yards to miles. Also, the miles used in the United States may be different from the miles used in

These sausage-shaped objects are bacteria, each about a micrometer long. They are shown here magnified about 100,000 times.

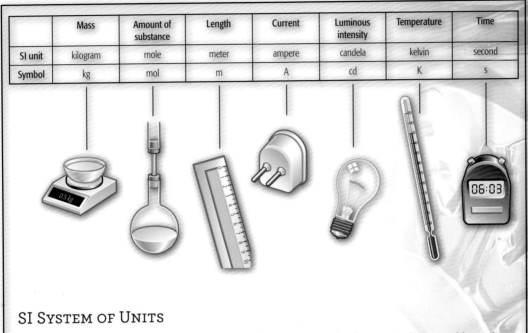

	Mass	Amount of substance	Length	Current	Luminous intensity	Temperature	Time
SI unit	kilogram	mole	meter	ampere	candela	kelvin	second
Symbol	kg	mol	m	A	cd	K	s

SI SYSTEM OF UNITS

Shown above are the seven base units of the SI system, which are supplemented by radians and steradians for measuring angles in advanced math (1 radian equals about 57 degrees). Among the important derived units are the hertz, used for measuring frequency; the newton, for measuring force; the ohm, volt, and watt used for measuring electrical resistance, voltage and power, respectively; and the joule, for measuring energy.

Finland or in China. Pints and gallons in the United States are different from British pints and gallons. 1 U.S. pint equals 0.473 liters, while 1 British pint equals 0.568 liters (the British pint is more than 1.2 times bigger than the U.S. pint). The British gallon is also 1.2 times larger than the U.S. gallon. Scientists get around these problems by having only one unit for length—the meter. Every length is measured in meters or in multiples of meters (for example, kilometers) or in submultiples of meters (for example, centimeters).

To make the multiples and submultiples there are a number of standard prefixes that go before the word for "kilo-" means "1,000 times." So 1 kilometer = 1,000 meters (written as 1 km = 1,000 m). In a similar way "centi-" means "1/100," so 1 centimeter (1 cm) = 1/100 meter (0.01 m). Thus the distance from Chicago to Los Angeles is about 1,740 km; the length of a new pencil is about 18 cm. There is a list of these prefixes on page 9.

OLD MEASURING INSTRUMENTS

The illustration below shows some old types of measuring instruments:
(a) Human forearm, about 0.5 meter long
(b) Simple balance for weighing
(c) Water clock for telling time
(d) Sundial for telling time of day
(e) Astrolabe for measuring angles of stars
(f) Hourglass for measuring elapsed time
(g) Micrometer for measuring small thicknesses
(h) Sextant for measuring the Sun's angle in the sky

SI AND METRIC SYSTEMS

The meter is a unit in the metric system. This system was invented in France about 200 years ago, when the meter was taken to be a ten-millionth of the distance around the world. The kilogram is also a metric unit. The metric system is used for everyday measurements in most European countries and is becoming increasingly common in the United States.

Science uses a version of the metric system called the SI system (so called after its French name, Système International d'Unités). This system has seven base units, shown at the top of page 7, and two supplementary and various derived units. There are 18 derived units, each with a special name and made from combinations of the seven base units. The base unit of mass is the kilogram (= 1,000 grams), chosen because the gram (equal to about 1/30 oz.) is too small for many measurements. Throughout this book we give measurements in SI units, usually with their customary equivalents following in parentheses.

METRIC PREFIXES

Prefix	Symbol	Multiple	Prefix	Symbol	Multiple
atto-	a	$\times 10^{-18}$	deca-	da	$\times 10$
femto-	f	$\times 10^{-15}$	hecto-	h	$\times 10^{2}$
pico-	p	$\times 10^{-12}$	kilo-	k	$\times 10^{3}$
nano-	n	$\times 10^{-9}$	mega-	M	$\times 10^{6}$
micro-	μ	$\times 10^{-6}$	giga-	G	$\times 10^{9}$
milli-	m	$\times 10^{-3}$	tera-	T	$\times 10^{12}$
centi-	c	$\times 10^{-2}$	peta-	P	$\times 10^{15}$
deci-	d	$\times 10^{-1}$	exa-	E	$\times 10^{18}$

Here are some examples:
picofarad (pF), equal to 10^{-12} farads, used to measure capacitance
nanometer (nm), equal to 10^{-9} meters, used to measure molecules
microampere (μA), equal to 10^{-6} amperes, used to measure nerve impulses
milligram (mg), equal to 10^{-3} grams, used to weigh out medicines
centiliter (cl), equal to 10^{-2} liters, used to measure wine
hectare (ha), equal to 10^{2} ares, used for areas of fields
kilovolt (kV), equal to 10^{3} volts, used for railroad voltages
megawatt (MW), equal to 10^{6} watts, used for a power-plant output
gigabyte (Gb), equal to 10^{9} bytes, used for computer storage capacity

POWERS OF TEN

When measurements are made using SI or metric units, some of the numbers become very large indeed. For example, the Earth is about 150 million km from the Sun, which in figures is 150,000,000 km. Standard form uses an index to express large numbers as powers of 10. For instance, $1,000 = 10^3$ and $1,000,000 = 10^6$. So the distance to the Sun is 1.5×10^8 km. A human hair is about a ten-thousandth of a meter across, or 0.0001 m. In standard form this is written as 1×10^{-4} m.

Atomic clocks keep time to an accuracy of better than 1 second in 30,000 years.

A high jumper clears the bar at a track-and-field contest. Athletes' achievements are measured in metric units. The world women's high jump record is more than 2 meters.

CHAPTER TWO
GRAVITY AND MASS

The mass of an object remains the same wherever it is on the Earth. It even stays the same if we send it to the Moon or launch it by rocket into outer space. But an object's weight can change depending on the local force of gravity.

Mass is a measure of the amount of matter in an object. That is why an object's mass always remains the same, wherever it is. But the weight of an object is the force acting on it by the gravitational attraction of the Earth (or any other nearby planetary body). As a result, an object's weight depends on its distance from the Earth. It is very slightly less at the top of a high mountain than at sea level. On the surface of the Moon the same object would weigh only about one-sixth of its weight on Earth. That is

SLOWING DOWN GRAVITY

To study a falling ball, Galileo slowed it down by rolling it along a slope. He measured how far the ball rolled in equal time intervals and found that speed increased uniformly with time.

0 1 2 3 Equal time intervals

4

5

0   2   4   6   8   10   12   14   16   18   20   22   24   26   28   Distance

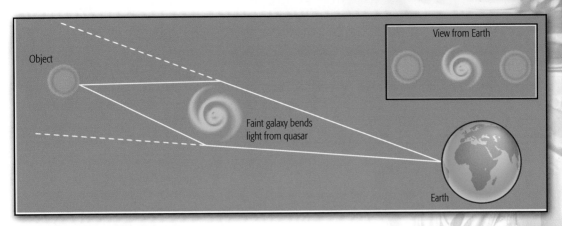

Object

View from Earth

Faint galaxy bends
light from quasar

Earth

Gravity and Light

A gravitational field can bend a beam of light. When light from a distant object passes on either side of a galaxy, the galaxy's powerful gravity bends the light rays. An observer on Earth sees two images of the same object, one on each side of the galaxy. (This diagram is not to scale!)

because the Moon's force of gravity is only one-sixth of the Earth's.

The scientific unit of mass is the kilogram (kg); the unit of weight is the newton (N). An object's weight is equal to its mass multiplied by the acceleration due to gravity (which is also called the acceleration of free fall). Because this equals 9.8 meters per second per second (9.8 m/s^2) at the surface of the Earth, there is a simple relationship between weight (in newtons) and mass (in kilograms):

$$weight = 9.8 \times mass$$

Thus a person whose mass is 50 kg weighs 490 newtons. The same person would weigh only 82 N in the Moon's lower gravity—and a huge 1,294 N on the giant planet Jupiter!

GALILEO

Galileo Galilei, to give him his full name, was an astronomer and physicist who was born in Pisa, Italy, in 1564. In physics one of his main studies had to do with gravity. Observing the swinging lamps in the cathedral at Pisa, he realized that the regular swinging motion of a pendulum might be used to regulate a clock. He studied falling objects by dropping weights from towers and rolling balls down inclined planes. In astronomy Galileo made one of the first telescopes, and with it he discovered craters on the Moon, sunspots, and four moons of Jupiter. He also backed Copernicus and said that the Earth orbits the Sun (not the other way around, as was then believed), which lies at the center of the Solar System.

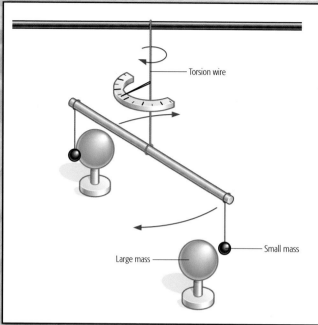

TORSION BALANCE

The English physicist Henry Cavendish made this apparatus in 1798. A gravitational force attracted two small balls toward two much more massive ones, causing twisting, or torsion, in the suspension. From the amount of twisting Cavendish calculated the value of the gravitational constant.

Torsion wire

Large mass

Small mass

CONVERSIONS

Scientists are always very careful to distinguish between mass and weight. But this difference is not so important in everyday life. In fact, for ordinary measurements we tend to use mass units to express weights. Thus we might buy

A weight lifter strains to lift heavy weights against the force of the Earth's gravity. He would find it much easier if he tried it on the Moon!

A space shuttle, with its huge fuel tanks and booster rockets, needs powerful rocket motors to lift it into space against the force of Earth's gravity.

5 kg of potatoes or 50 kg of coal and express the weight of the 490-newton person as 50 kg.

Sometimes we need to convert from one system of mass/weight to the other system. To convert from kilograms to pounds, multiply by 2.2 (thus 50 kg = 110 lb). To convert the other way, from pounds to kilograms, divide by 2.2.

DIFFERENT BALANCES

The earliest weighing machines resembled the one pictured in the middle of page 8. This type, called a balance, is still used throughout science and industry. It consists of a horizontal beam pivoted at its center so that it balances—hence the name! A pan hangs from each end of the beam. To weigh out a particular quantity, say a kilogram of rice, a mass of 1 kilogram is put on one pan. Rice is then poured onto the other pan until the beam is again horizontal—until it balances. In this manner quantities of materials can be weighed out. To find the weight of a particular quantity, it is put in one pan, and known weights are added to the

Recipes often call for certain weights of ingredients, which can be found with a kitchen scale.

other pan until it balances. So to use the device for weighing things you need a set of known weights.

Of course, such a "weighing" exercise as this doesn't really find the weight of anything: what it does is to manipulate masses. This type of balance would work just as well on the Moon because it actually compares masses. But a spring balance is different. Most kitchen scales are of this type, with a vertical coiled spring and a pan on top that compresses the spring. A pointer that is worked by the movement of the spring indicates weights on a marked dial.

What this device does is to measure the effect of the force of gravity on an object's mass. It is therefore a force meter; similar devices used in physics laboratories are called newton meters. The spring balance really does measure weight and would register only a sixth of an object's "Earth weight" if the same object were weighed with it on the Moon.

GRAVITATIONAL PULL

Every object is attracted toward every other object by a force known as gravitation, which arises because objects have mass. The force of gravity is simply the force of attraction between an object and the much more massive Earth. When you drop something, it is this force that makes it fall to the ground. The actual size of the force between any two objects depends on their masses and their distance apart. In mathematical terms we say the force is proportional to the product of the masses divided by the square of the distance between them. As a result, the closer they are together, the stronger is the force of attraction between them. If the masses are m_1 and m_2, and the distance between them is d, the force F between them can be expressed as

$$F = G \frac{m_1 \times m_2}{d^2}$$

where G is the gravitational constant. This equation is an example of an inverse square law, so called because the strength of some quantity (here, force) gets less with the square of the distance from a particular point.

An astronaut who weighed 180 pounds on Earth would only weigh about 1/6 of that, or about 30 pounds, on the Moon.

CHAPTER THREE

ACCELERATION AND RESISTANCE

When an object falls under the force of gravity, does it fall at a constant speed, or does it get faster and faster? In other words, does it accelerate? This question puzzled early scientists until Galileo did some experiments to find the answer.

Galileo's experiment illustrated on page 12 shows how he found that the speed of a ball rolling down a slope continues to increase—in other words, it accelerates. Galileo also found that every freely falling object has the same acceleration. Now called the acceleration due to gravity, it has the value 9.8 m/s² (32 ft/s²).

According to tradition, Galileo also tried to measure the acceleration of a cannonball dropped off the top of the Leaning Tower of Pisa. The illustration on the left shows what the results would have been if he had a way of making such measurements (which he did not). The cannonball would have reached a speed of 9.8 m/s (32 ft/s) after 1 second, a speed of 19.6 m/s (64 ft/s) after 2 seconds, and so on. The speed increases, but the acceleration is unchanging.

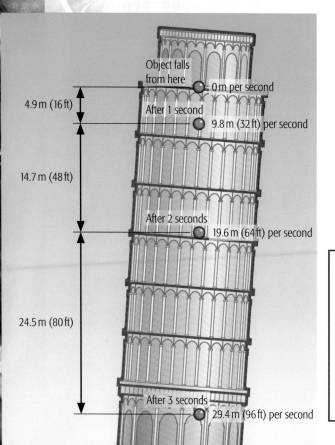

- Object falls from here — 0 m per second
- 4.9 m (16 ft)
- After 1 second — 9.8 m (32 ft) per second
- 14.7 m (48 ft)
- After 2 seconds — 19.6 m (64 ft) per second
- 24.5 m (80 ft)
- After 3 seconds — 29.4 m (96 ft) per second

ACCELERATION DUE TO GRAVITY

The figures show how an object would fall in the first 3 seconds after being dropped from the Leaning Tower of Pisa. Its speed increases, but its acceleration is constant at 9.8 m/s² (32 ft/s²).

USING DRAG

In practice, an object falling in air does not keep getting faster and faster. The air resists the downward movement of the object, and this air resistance acts as an upward force called drag. The drag increases as the object's speed increases, so that eventually the object can go no faster. Most falling objects reach a constant terminal speed of about 54 m/s (177 ft/s or about 120 mph). Think of the damage hailstones could do if they fell any faster!

Drag is larger on an object with a large area than it is on one with a small area. This is the principle of a parachute, which when open gives a falling human a terminal speed of 6.3 m/s (nearly 21 ft/s or 14 mph). That is the speed at which a parachutist hits the ground. You can prove the principle with a sheet of paper. Drop it, and it flutters to the ground because of the high drag acting on it. But crumple it into a tight ball, and you will find that it falls much quicker because there is much less drag.

ACCELERATION OF FREE FALL

An object falling under the force of gravity is said to be in free fall (and acceleration due to gravity is also known as acceleration of free fall). It has the symbol g, and it crops up in many of the physical formulas that have to do with mechanics, such as the formula for calculating the time of a pendulum's swing (see page 37) and equations for calculating pressures under water.

Skydivers reach their terminal speed (about 54 m/s) after about 12 seconds. They then fall at this constant speed until they open their parachutes and rapidly decelerate, reaching the ground at a speed of 6.3 m/s.

CHAPTER FOUR

QUANTITY AND DIRECTION

Air-traffic controllers use vectors to indicate the positions of airplanes. They need to known how far away the airplanes are and in what direction.

Most quantities in physics are expressed as a number and some unit, such as 25 kg or 110 volts. These last examples are called scalars. But what is the difference between a speed of 50 km/h and a velocity of 50 km/h in the direction of Chicago? The first (speed) is a scalar, but the second (velocity) is a vector quantity.

A vector quantity always has its direction specified, whereas a scalar is a pure number. A given quantity can be either, and sometimes the difference is very important. If you told some shipwrecked sailors on a life raft that there was an island only 3 kilometers away, they might be relieved. But it would be much more useful for

TRIANGLES AND PARALLELOGRAMS

The triangle of vectors (above) shows how to add vectors, in this case two forces. The effect of combining a force F1 in one direction and another force F2 in a different direction (the lengths of the arrows indicate the sizes of the forces) is called the resultant. The third side of the triangle shows the resultant's size and direction.

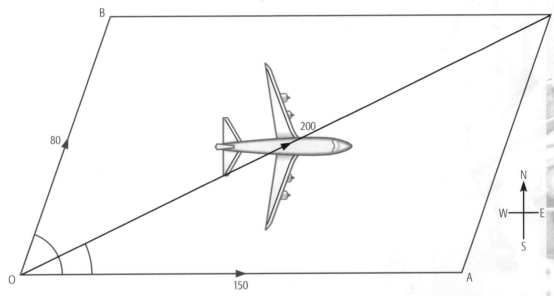

An airplane navigator wants to fly a plane 200 km from O to C. But there is a northerly wind along the line from O to B. What course should the navigator set? The correct course is due east, toward A. The parallelogram of vectors shows that the plane will actually fly along the line from O to C, as required.

them to know that there was an island 3 kilometers away to the north. They would then know which way to paddle the life raft. We call "3 kilometers away" a scalar quantity; "3 kilometers away to the north" is a vector. Several quantities in physics are vectors. They include velocity, acceleration, and most forces.

ADDING QUANTITIES

Adding scalar quantities is easy as long as you can do simple math. A piece of string 3 meters long added to a piece 4 meters long gives a total length of 7 meters of string (ignoring the string used to tie the knot).

But adding vectors is trickier. If you push a cart 30 meters to the east and then 40 meters to the south, where does the cart end up? The answer is 50 meters away from where you started, in a more or less south-easterly direction. Notice that the cart does not finish up 70 meters away, which is the result you would get if you merely added the two distances.

TRIANGLE OF VECTORS

One way of adding vectors is to draw a plan. Make the length of a line stand for the size of the vector, and draw it in the correct direction. Then, from the end of the first line draw a second line in the direction of the second vector, again with length standing for size. A line drawn between the beginning of the first line and the end of the second one represents the sum of the vectors and its direction. The construction you have made is called a triangle of vectors.

A compass uses Earth's magnetic field to align itself to the Earth's magnetic poles and give direction.

Understanding vectors is an important part of learning to read maps.

CHAPTER FIVE

LAWS OF MOTION

Force is what makes a thing move or stops it. The ease with which something moves depends on its mass. A moving object has a certain speed, and if its speed changes it accelerates. Force, mass, and acceleration are interconnected.

Force can make things move, stop moving, move faster or slower, or change the direction in which they move. It can also make things change shape, perhaps by squeezing them or stretching them. If you stretch a rubber band or snap a pencil you are using force. Even a humble paper clip exerts a force when it holds two pieces of paper together.

All the forces mentioned so far have to do with objects in contact with one another. But there are other forces that act at a distance. As we saw earlier, gravity is a force that pulls things down to the surface of the Earth.

A magnet exerts a force when it picks up

When the hockey player hits the puck, it skates across the ice and—according to Newton's laws—would go on forever if the force of friction did not slow it down.

Reaction

Action

ACTION AND REACTION

A person firing a rifle demonstrates the third law of motion. When the rifle is fired, a force (the action) speeds the bullet forward. At the same time the shooter feels a sudden recoil (the reaction) as the rifle is pushed backward.

an iron nail. There are also forces that act between electric charges. In fact, nearly all of physics is concerned with forces of one sort or another. But forces are most obvious when they have to do with movement, with what scientists call motion.

FORCE AND FRICTION

If you roll a ball along the ground, it does not keep on rolling forever but soon slows down and stops. Have you ever wondered why? In the 17th century the English scientist Isaac Newton wondered why and came up

A hammer exerts a force on a nail as it strikes. However, the nail also exerts a force on the hammer.

ISAAC NEWTON

Sir Isaac Newton (1642–1727) was an English mathematician, astronomer, and physicist. He was born at Woolsthorpe, in Lincolnshire, and in 1661 went to study at Cambridge University. In 1669 he became professor of mathematics there. In mathematics Newton developed calculus, a system that can deal with changing quantities. In astronomy he made one of the first reflecting telescopes and worked out how the Moon orbits the Earth. To do this, he used the law of gravitation, one of his major contributions to physics. He studied light and produced the Sun's spectrum by passing sunlight through a glass prism. He also formulated his three famous laws of motion. In 1705 he became the first scientist ever to be knighted. He is buried in Westminster Abbey and is regarded as one of the world's greatest scientists.

with a set of rules that apply to all moving objects. Together, these rules are now known as Newton's laws of motion.

The first law states that an object at rest will stay at rest, or a moving object will go on moving, unless a force acts on it. So according to Newton, our ball started rolling because we gave it a push—we applied a force. It then stopped rolling because it was acted on by another force. In this case the second force was friction between the ball and the ground.

That is why a ball will roll farther on a smooth surface than it will on a rough one—try rolling a marble across a wooden floor (low friction) and across a carpet (high friction).

Newton's second law of motion involves acceleration, which is the rate at which a moving object changes speed. The law says that the force acting on an object is equal to its mass multiplied by its acceleration. So if you give something a push (apply a force), it will move off at a certain speed. But if you want it to move faster and faster, you have to keep on applying force. A spacecraft returning to the Earth from the Moon travels at a fairly constant speed until it gets close to the Earth. Then the Earth's gravity (a

(a)

Motor on

Forward push

A drag racing car accelerates to speeds of up to 400 km/h from a standing start over a distance of just 400 meters (the world record is more than 500 km/h).

STARTING AND STOPPING

When the drag racing car starts (a), the forward push of the car's motor has to overcome friction. During the run (b) the car continues to accelerate as the motor continues to provide forward force. At the end of the run (c) the driver turns off the motor and releases a parachute to provide even more wind resistance and slow down the car until it comes to a standstill.

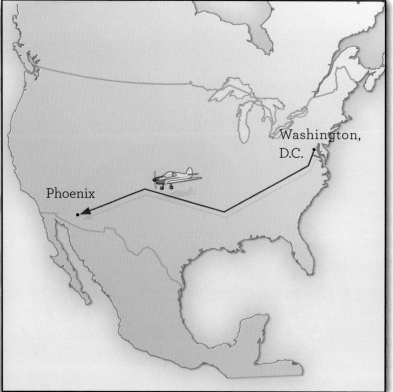

Washington, D.C.

Phoenix

SPEED AND VELOCITY

An airplane flies from Washington, D.C., to Phoenix at a constant speed, but its velocity changes every time it changes direction.

force) has more effect and makes it accelerate. Strictly speaking, we should use the term velocity instead of speed (velocity is speed in a specified direction).

The third law of motion concerns two objects. It states that when one object exerts a force on another, the second object exerts the same force on the first but in the opposite direction. The first force is an action and the second a reaction, and the law is sometimes stated as "action and reaction are equal and opposite."

When we drop a book, gravity is the action force that makes it fall. There is also an equal reaction force between the book and the Earth, but it is undetectable because the mass of the Earth is huge compared with that of the book. The forces between the Earth and the Moon are easier to understand. The Earth's gravity pulls on the Moon and keeps it in orbit. The Moon's gravity pulls on the water in the Earth's oceans and causes the daily tides.

Another example of the third law is the principle of the rocket. The hot burning gases in a rocket expand and push in all directions. Those that push on the closed front end of the rocket are balanced by a reaction, which acts in the opposite direction and propels the rocket along. For this reason a rocket is known technically as a type of reaction motor.

The force of the Moon's gravity on Earth causes high and low tides in the ocean. During high tide, these tidal pools are covered with water. During low tide, some water and sea creatures are left in the pools.

MOVEMENT AND MOMENTUM

A heavy object is more difficult to start moving than a lighter one. That is because of its mass or inertia. Inertia can be thought of as an object's reluctance to move. If you are traveling in an automobile and the driver brakes suddenly, it is your inertia that makes you keep moving unless held back by a seat belt.

Once an object is moving, it has momentum, which is equal to its mass multiplied by its velocity. The more massive a moving object is, or the faster it moves, the greater is its momentum. It is easy to demonstrate the difference between inertia and momentum. If you carefully place a brick on your foot, it is difficult to raise your toes—that's inertia. But if you dropped the brick on your foot, it would do a lot of damage—that's momentum!

A small object moving very fast can have more momentum than a massive object moving slowly. For example, a bullet fired from a Magnum revolver can have enough momentum to stop a moving automobile because the bullet's momentum is greater than that of the car.

A car seat keeps a child's momentum from throwing him forward during a sudden stop or accident.

A good understanding of physics and mathematics is very useful during a game of pool.

Newton's second and third laws of motion predict that when two objects bump into each other, their total momentum after impact is the same as it was before impact. This statement is often called the principle of conservation of momentum.

It accounts for various things in everyday life, particularly in sports. People playing pool or hockey make unconscious use of the conservation of momentum when they strike a ball or the puck. When a rider's horse refuses to jump over a fence, the horse stops, but momentum keeps the rider going, sometimes with a painful result.

Like velocity, acceleration is a vector quantity. It is specified by a number (how large it is) and a direction. An example of a velocity is "5 meters per second northward." Acceleration is measured in units such as meters per second per second. Speed, on the other hand, is a scalar quantity. It is stated merely as a number and unit with no direction, such as "500 km/h."

CHAPTER SIX

CIRCULAR MOTION

So far we have considered mainly objects moving in straight lines and the various forces that can act on them. Slightly different rules apply if an object is moving in a curved path, particularly if it is moving around and around in a circle.

We are going to begin with a very difficult idea. When an object moves in a straight line, the only way it can accelerate (or decelerate) is by changing its speed—by going faster (or slower). But we know from chapter four that velocity is a vector quantity. So if an object is moving at a certain speed in a certain direction (that is, if it has a

People on this carnival ride feel as though they are being flung outward. In fact, their velocity constantly changes as they go around in a circle.

certain velocity), it can be acted on by a force—for example, by giving it a sideways push—that changes its direction without changing its speed. As a result, its velocity changes. And that amounts to saying that it undergoes acceleration, which after all is defined as change in velocity divided by time. So, although it might seem unlikely at first, it is quite possible for something to be accelerating without its speed changing.

Now think of a stone tied to the end of a piece of string and whirled around your head in a horizontal circle. Its speed is constant; but because its direction is continuously changing, it is always accelerating. The force that accelerates the stone is the pull in the string. Its direction is at right angles to the direction of

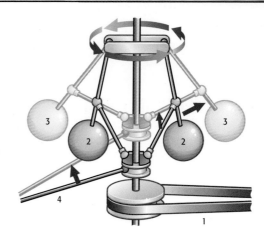

FEEDBACK CONTROL

A mechanism for controlling the speed of an engine, called a governor, makes use of circular motion. The vertical shaft is turned by a belt (1) driven by the machine. As it turns, the weights (2), attached at the top of the shaft, go around and rise (3). This action raises the rod (4), which reduces the power supply to the engine and slows it down. As it slows, the weights fall and so increase the power to the engine.

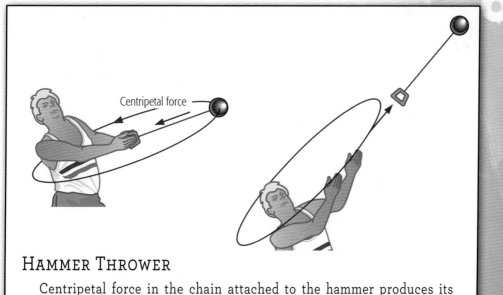

Centripetal force

HAMMER THROWER

Centripetal force in the chain attached to the hammer produces its acceleration in a circle. When the thrower lets go, the hammer flies off in the direction it was traveling at the instant it was released.

the stone at any instant, directed inward toward the center of the circle. Physicists call it centripetal force.

OBJECTS IN ORBIT

The English scientist Isaac Newton worked out that a force is involved in keeping an object moving in a circle around another object. So what is the force that keeps the Moon orbiting the Earth? It is the force of gravity between the Earth and the Moon. In a way, the Moon is always falling in a circle toward the Earth. But it keeps falling past and going around again—or at least it has for the last 4 billion years or so!

Artificial satellites orbiting the Moon, Earth, or another planet act in the same way under the gravitational attraction of the body that they orbit. To lift an orbiting satellite into a higher orbit, it has to be given more speed (by firing its rocket motors). When a satellite slows down, perhaps because of friction between it and the outer layers of the Earth's atmosphere, it can no longer stay in its orbit and soon spirals down toward the Earth.

The rings around the planet Saturn consist of millions of orbiting icy particles held in position by the planet's gravitational field.

There are thousands of manmade objects in orbit around Earth at any given time.

CHAPTER SEVEN

PENDULUMS AND CLOCKS

A pendulum swings through an arc of a circle, with the suspension point at the center of the circle. Two quantities that can be varied are the length of the pendulum and the mass of the pendulum bob. Only one of them affects the time of the swing.

There is a traditional story about the first person to observe the perfectly regular swing of a pendulum—one of many anecdotes told about the Italian scientist Galileo. In 1602, while sitting in the cathedral at Pisa, he noticed the ceiling lamps swinging in the breeze. He did not have a watch (watches had not yet been invented), so he timed the swings using his heartbeat by feeling the pulse in his wrist.

Galileo found that each lamp swung at a regular pace. He also noticed that lamps on

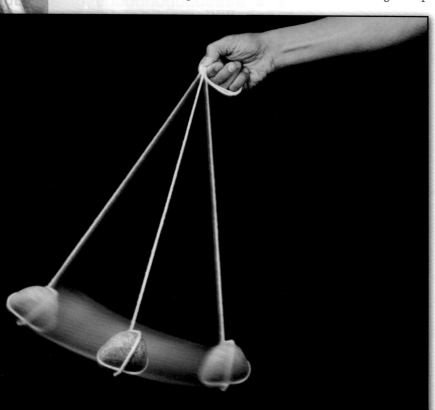

A pendulum is momentarily stationary every time it changes direction at the end of each swing.

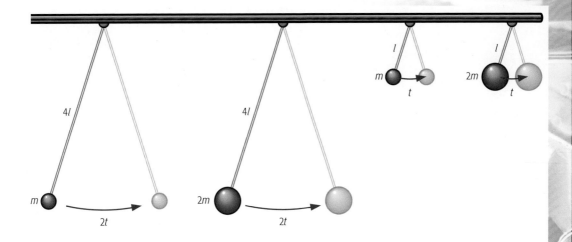

LENGTH AND MASS

The left-hand pair of pendulums have a cord $4l$ long. The time of the swing is $2t$, which does not change even when the mass is doubled from m to $2m$. But shortening the cord to l (right-hand pair) halves the time of swing to t.

long chains swung more slowly than did lamps on short chains. He also wondered whether the heavy lamps swung more slowly than the lighter ones. He could not weigh the lamps, so he did some experiments.

The results of Galileo's experiments with pendulums are illustrated above. He found that changing the mass of the bob (the weight at the end of the cord) had no effect on the time of the swing as long as the pendulum swung through only small angles. But changing the length of the cord did change the time of the swing. This time period was halved when he shortened the cord to one-fourth of its former length.

TIME EQUATION

Galileo found that the time for a pendulum's complete swing—that is, from one side, across to the other side, and back again—is proportional to the square root of the pendulum's length. The actual relationship is given by the equation

$$t = 2\pi \sqrt{\frac{l}{g}}$$

where t is the time and l is the length of the cord. Notice that the equation has two other symbols. One is π (pi), which often turns up when circles are involved, and the other symbol is g, the acceleration due to gravity.

PRACTICAL USES

The first important application of the pendulum was to regulate the mechanism of a clock. Galileo suggested this, but the Dutch scientist Christiaan Huygens built the first practical pendulum clocks in 1656. The swinging pendulum regulated an escapement, which was a wheel and ratchet arrangement that allowed other wheels to turn slowly, driven by a falling weight or by a spring.

Before the invention of clocks that kept exact time, many people estimated the hour by using sundials. Sundials use shadows cast by the Sun to show the time of day.

While many modern clocks no longer use pendulums, watching a grandfather clock is a great way to see a pendulum in action.

CHAPTER EIGHT

ALL ABOUT ENERGY

Energy, work, and power are sometimes confused. Energy is the ability to do work; work results when a force acts over a distance; and power is the rate of doing work. So we will begin with energy, of which there are various kinds.

When asked to do a chore at the end of a tiring day, we may say, "I can't—I don't have the energy." This is a fairly accurate statement, scientifically speaking. Energy is something that, possessed by something else, enables it to do work. As we will see, there are various kinds of energy. We cannot make it or destroy it, which is called the principle of conservation of energy. But we can use energy, and in doing so we change it from one of its forms to another form.

The energy we use doing work comes from the food we eat. Food is essentially a mixture of chemicals. The processes of digestion change them into other chemicals, such as the high-energy sugar glucose. When we do work, our muscles use up glucose to provide energy.

The water stored behind the dam represents a huge reserve of potential energy. As the water falls, the potential energy is converted to kinetic energy that can be made to do work by turning turbine blades.

FORMS OF ENERGY

Potential energy is energy that something has because of its position. A book on a shelf, for example, has energy stored in it as potential energy. It may look the same as a book on the floor; but if it is knocked off the shelf, the falling book can be made to do work. Imagine tying a string to the book and attaching the other end to a nearby vase. Knock the book off the shelf, and watch it do work on the vase! The water stored in a reservoir behind a dam has potential energy that can do work turning turbines to make electricity.

Strain energy is similar in some ways. When you wind up a clock or pull a bow, you strain the material of the spring or the bow and store energy in it. The clock spring slowly unwinds to work the clock, and the bow very rapidly straightens to speed an arrow to its target.

Kinetic energy is the energy of motion, so it is the form of energy possessed by anything that is moving. A swinging hammer has kinetic energy that can do the work of knocking a nail into a lump of wood. A speeding truck has lots of kinetic energy, which is why it can cause so much damage if it accidentally crashes into something.

KINDS OF ENERGY

Nine different kinds of energy are illustrated here, from the potential energy of the weights wound up in the clock to the awesome nuclear energy of an exploding atomic bomb, which releases vast quantities of heat, light, and sound.

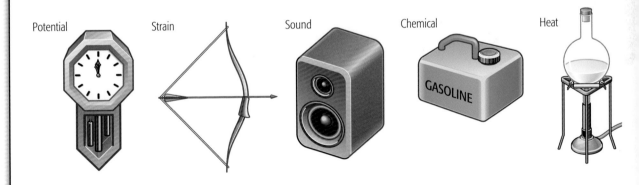

Potential Strain Sound Chemical Heat

Light Electrical Kinetic Nuclear

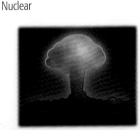

Heat and light are also forms of energy. Anything that is hot possesses heat energy that can be made to do work in machines such as steam turbines and automobile engines. Green plants use light energy to combine carbon dioxide and water to form sugar and oxygen in the process known as photosynthesis, and light brings about other chemical reactions utilized in photography. The energy of the light in a laser beam is great enough to cut through metal.

Electrical energy is one of the most familiar types of energy. It is produced by batteries and by generators in power plants, and can be made to do all kinds of work from, for example, powering flashlights to driving railroad locomotives.

Sound is a form of energy that is seldom used directly for its energy, although ultrasound is used in medicine and industry to break up kidney stones and cut metals. Prolonged exposure to loud sounds can damage human hearing, sometimes permanently.

The chemical energy locked up in fuels is released when the fuels are burned to produce heat or light. Chemical energy is also released in batteries (but more slowly), where it is converted into electricity.

The final type of energy we need to know about is nuclear energy. It is produced by changes that take place in the nuclei of atoms. Energy is released in fission reactions when large nulcei (such as uranium) split into smaller ones. Nuclear energy also comes from fusion reactions in which light nuclei such as hydrogen nuclei combine to form heavier ones. Fusion reactions take place at the heart of the Sun and other stars, as well as in the hydrogen bomb.

CHANGING FORMS

We noted earlier than energy cannot be created or destroyed, merely changed from one form into another. A few examples should illustrate this point. The pendulum (pages 36–37) is an energy converter. When the pendulum bob is at one end of its swing it has potential energy (because of its position). As it swings across it gains kinetic energy (because it is moving). The potential energy is converted to kinetic energy, which is changed back to potential energy at the other end of the swing.

A speeding bullet also has kinetic energy. When it hits a hard target such as a wall, it stops, and

A ball rolling back and forth in a basin switches between having all potential energy (at the highest positions) and all kinetic energy (at the lowest position).

the kinetic energy is converted into heat energy, as well as some sound energy. When a meteorite enters the Earth's atmosphere, friction with the air heats it up (heat energy), and it ionizes atoms in the atmosphere, creating a brief streak of light (light energy), which we see as a falling star. The food we eat has chemical energy stored in it. This energy drives our body processes, keeps us warm, and is used up in our muscles whenever we do physical work.

MEASURING ENERGY AND WORK

The energy content of food is generally measured in joules (or calories). And the joule is the unit used for measuring every other form of energy—for example, heat and mechanical energy. It is possible to compare energy sources in terms of joules. The joule is also the unit for measuring work. In fact, 1 joule is equal to a force of 1 newton moving through a distance of 1 meter. Whenever a force moves something, work is done. For example, if you pick up off the floor a book weighing 20 newtons (i.e., it has a mass of about 2 kg) and place it on a shelf 0.5 m high, the work done by your muscles is 20 × 0.5 = 10 joules. If you carry three books up a flight of stairs 4 meters high, the work done is 60 × 4 = 240 joules—much more tiring!

MEASURING POWER

Power is the rate of doing work. If you carried those three books upstairs in 12 seconds, the power would be 240 ÷ 12 = 20 joules per second. But if you ran up the stairs in just 4 seconds, the power would be 240 ÷ 4 = 60 joules per second. (Both of these sums neglect the power that is

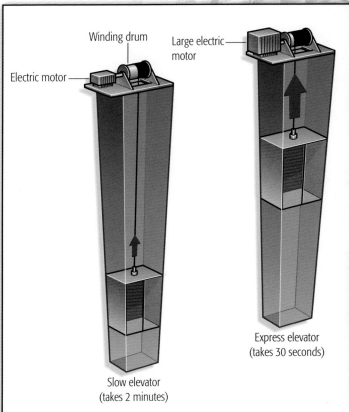

Winding drum

Electric motor

Large electric motor

Express elevator
(takes 30 seconds)

Slow elevator
(takes 2 minutes)

Slow and Fast Elevators

If these two elevators carry the same numbers of passengers, the express elevator needs four times as much power to move four times as fast as the slow elevator. It therefore needs a much larger electric motor to power its winding drum.

used in lifting you upstairs.) Although the calculations here give power in joules per second, in physics power has its own unit, the watt (1 watt = 1 joule per second), named after the Scottish engineer James Watt. So in your run upstairs you converted energy at 60 watts—about the same as a dim electric lightbulb.

Like the ball in the basin on page 42, the people on the roller coaster switch between having mostly potential energy to mostly kinetic energy. They do retain some kinetic energy at the top of the ride because they keep moving.

An archer stretches her bow and takes aim, about to convert the strain energy stored in the bow into the kinetic energy of a speeding arrow.

The sudden destructive release of chemical energy is evident in this accidental detonation of blasting explosives.

CHAPTER NINE

BALANCING FORCES

Normally, when a force acts on an object it makes it move in a straight line in the direction of the force. But in certain circumstances a force may have no effect at all, or cause the object to move in the arc of a circle, or even make it fall over.

The effect of a force on an object depends on how stable the object is. A cubical box on a table just sits there. It is perfectly stable and shows no tendency to move. If you tilt it slightly, raising one edge off the table, then let it go, it sits back down on the table. In scientific terms it is said to be in stable equilibrium.

A cylinder on its side is slightly different. It will stay where it is put; but if given a slight push, it will roll along. It is in neutral equilibrium. But a narrow cylinder balanced on one end is different. Give it the slightest sideways tilt, and it topples over. It is in unstable equilibrium.

This mobile resembles two seesaws joined together.

Seesaws, like the one seen here, are often called teeter-totters.

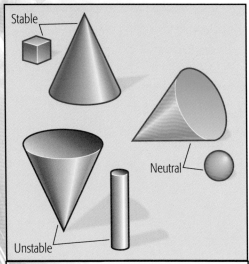

Stable

Neutral

Unstable

EQUILIBRIUM

The cube and the cone on its base are both in stable equilibrium, and each falls back onto its base if tilted. The ball and the cone on its side are both in neutral equilibrium and can roll. The cone on its point and the narrow cylinder are both in unstable equilibrium, and they topple if tilted far enough sideways.

CONCENTRATED MASS

The point at which all of an object's mass appears to be concentrated is called its center of gravity (also sometimes called center of mass). In the cubical box the center of gravity is right at the center. If you tilt the box, its center of gravity rises slightly. In the cylinder on its side the center of gravity is halfway along its axis (the line joining the centers of each end). When the cylinder rolls, its center of gravity moves sideways but does not move farther up or down.

The same cylinder standing on end has its center of gravity in the same place—halfway along its central axis. But this time, when the cylinder is tilted sideways, the center of gravity moves down slightly, and a vertical line through it meets the table at a position outside the cylinder's base. This combination of circumstances makes the cylinder unstable, and it falls over.

So, the stability of an object depends on what happens to its center of gravity when it is tilted. If the center moves up, the object is in stable equilibrium. If the center moves sideways, it is in neutral equilibrium. But if the center moves down, the object is in unstable equilibrium.

TURNING MOMENTS

A seesaw represents a different kind of equilibrium. Think of a seesaw pivoted at its center. It balances on the pivot (which is called a fulcrum in physics) because there are equal weights on either side. But add unequal weights to each side—say a child at the end of one side and an adult at the end of the other—and the seesaw tips downward on the heavier side. The unequal forces (the weights of the people are forces) produce

Child   Child
Fulcrum

Child   Adult

Child   Adult

Simple Seesaw

A seesaw is a simple example of turning moments. Children of equal weight balance at equal distances from the pivot. For an adult to have a ride, he or she has to sit closer to the pivot.

Tightrope walkers often hold their arms out or carry a long pole across their bodies to shift their center of gravity and make themselves more stable.

a turning effect. This effect is called a turning moment, and its size is equal to the force multiplied by its distance from the fulcrum.

So to balance the seesaw with the child and the adult, we have to make the turning moments the same. The only way to do this is for the adult to move nearer the fulcrum so that the adult's weight multiplied by his distance to the fulcrum is the same as the product of the child's weight and her distance to the fulcrum.

By the way, because a turning moment is equal to a force (measured in newtons, N) multiplied by a distance (measured in meters, m), its units are newton meters, written as Nm. A monkey wrench is a good example of a practical use of turning moments. When changing a wheel on a car with a flat tire, it is not possible to turn the wheel nuts using fingers—they are not strong enough. But using a wrench makes it easy because a force of 100 N applied at right angles to the handle of a wrench 25 cm long produces a turning moment of 100 × 0.25 = 25 Nm. The crank between the pedal of a bicycle and the chain wheel acts in a similar way to produce rotation. You also use a turning moment whenever you open a door. It takes more force to open a short wide door than a tall narrow one because the distance from the handle to the hinges is greater.

COUPLING FORCES

If there are two turning moments acting at the same point, the combined effect of both forces is called a couple. A familiar example is a faucet, which is turned by applying one moment on one side and an equal and opposite moment on the other side. Engineers sometimes use a long cylindrical wrench, called a socket wrench, for undoing stubborn nuts. It has a rod, termed a tommy bar, through one end of the cylinder. The other end goes over the nut, and the engineer applies a turning force to each end of the tommy bar. The turning effect of the couple unscrews the nut. A screwdriver is another example of a tool that uses couples. A screwdriver with a fat handle produces a greater couple and more turning force than one with a thin handle.

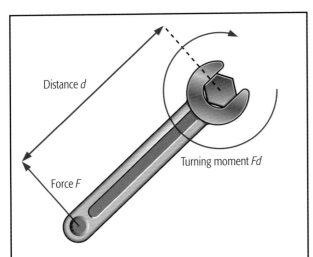

Distance *d*

Force *F*

Turning moment *Fd*

WRENCH AROUND

Applying a force *F* to the handle of a wrench at a distance *d* from the nut produces a turning moment *Fd*, also known as a torque.

CHAPTER TEN

LEVERS IN ACTION

A lever is probably the simplest kind of machine, which we can define as any device that provides a mechanical advantage. But even though they are simple, there are three very different kinds of lever, which have dozens of applications.

The Greek scientist Archimedes is supposed to have said, "Give me a lever long enough and somewhere to stand, and I will move the Earth." He certainly did make extensive use of levers in the various ingenious machines he designed for his patron, the King of Syracuse.

TYPES OF LEVERS

All kinds of lever have several things in common. They all involve a force, called the effort, that moves a load, making use of a pivot, or fulcrum. Archimedes' Earth-moving lever was a Class 1 lever, which works like a crowbar. Scissors or shears make use of a pair of Class 1 levers. The effort and load act in the same direction on opposite sides of the fulcrum (see the illustration on the opposite page).

In a Class 2 lever the effort and load are on the same side of the fulcrum and act in opposite directions. The load is

A pole-vaulter's pole acts as a lever to lift her into the air. The vaulter also gets help from the springiness of the pole.

Class 1 lever

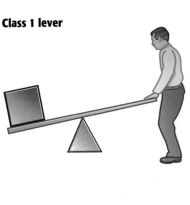

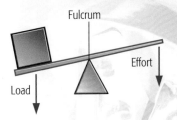

Class 2 lever

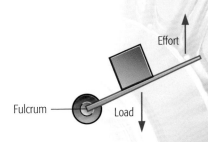

Class 3 lever

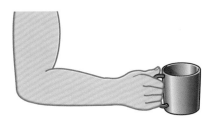

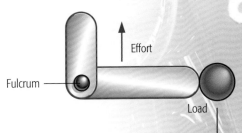

THREE CLASSES OF LEVER

The three classes of lever are Class 1, with load and effort on opposite sides of the fulcrum; Class 2, with load and effort on the same side but the load nearer the fulcrum; and Class 3, with load and effort again on the same side but the effort nearer the fulcrum.

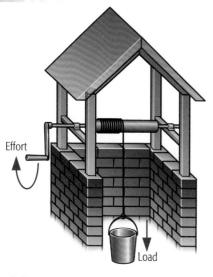

WHEEL AND AXLE

A wheel and axle are used in a windlass for raising a bucket from a well. This can provide a large mechanical advantage.

nearer the fulcrum than the effort. A wheelbarrow is an example of a Class 2 lever.

Finally, a Class 3 lever also has the effort and the load on the same side and acting in opposite directions. But this time the effort is nearer the fulcrum than the load is. The way your forearm works when you pick up something and the way tweezers and tongs work are examples of Class 3 levers in action. In fact, all movements of jointed bones in our bodies involve levers of one type or another.

LOAD, EFFORT, AND FULCRUM

In a Class 1 lever, if the distance from the effort to the fulcrum is greater than the distance from the load to the fulcrum, then a small effort can move a large load. We say that the lever provides a mechanical

DUMP TRUCK

The hydraulic mechanism of this dump truck is an example of a Class 2 lever. Compare it with the wheelbarrow on page 53.

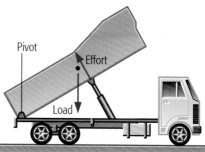

advantage, which is defined as the load (output force) divided by the effort (input force). This ratio is also sometimes called the force ratio, and for a Class 1 lever it is equal to the distance from the effort to the fulcrum divided by the distance from the load to the fulcrum. It also equals the distance the effort moves divided by the distance the load moves.

For a lever or any other kind of machine to be useful, the mechanical advantage must be greater than 1. Imagine trying to pry the lid off a tin of paint using a coin as a kind of short crowbar. It acts as a Class 1 lever with a mechanical advantage of about 4. (Because mechanical advantage is a ratio of two forces, it is a pure number and has no units.) If this is not enough to remove the lid, you can greatly increase the mechanical advantage by using a screwdriver to pry off the lid—like a long crowbar. This will provide a mechanical advantage of up to 30, which should be more than enough to open it. The illustrations in this chapter show other examples of various levers in action.

CONTINUOUS EFFORT

A windlass is a device that uses a handle to turn a cylindrical drum to wind a bucket up from a well. A capstan used to pull up the anchor chain on a ship is another example. In scientific terms such a device is called a wheel and axle. It is a variety of Class 1 lever in which the effort can be applied continuously.

The input force is applied at the rim of the wheel, and the output force acts at the rim of the axle. If the wheel has

The corkscrew also employs a pair of Class 1 levers. The load is very close to the fulcrum, producing a large mechanical advantage that should shift the most stubborn cork.

a radius of R units and the axle has a radius of r units, the mechanical advantage is R divided by r. A car's steering wheel is another everyday example of a wheel and axle.

ACHIEVING EFFICENCY

All these devices that use levers are examples of simple machines. Some perform better than others—that is, some machines are more efficient than others. Efficiency is the energy (or power) produced by a machine, the useful work done, divided by the energy (or power) it consumes. It is usually expressed as a percentage and is always less than 100 percent since no machine is perfect.

In practice there is usually a difference between any machine's theoretical mechanical advantage and its actual mechanical advantage. The ratio of these two—actual divided by theorectical—is also a measure of efficiency. A simple Class 1 lever is one of the most efficient machines, with an efficiency approaching 100 percent. Other simple machines, such as a screw (see page 58), are extremely inefficient.

A pair of garden shears, like scissors, consists of a pair of Class 1 levers working together. The longer the handles, the greater the mechanical advantage.

CHAPTER ELEVEN

INCLINES, WEDGES, AND SCREWS

It is much easier to push a load up a slope than to lift it directly upward. The slope is called an inclined plane, and it is another example of a simple machine that provides a mechanical advantage. Without it the ancient Egyptians could not have built the pyramids, and screws and bolts would not work.

Given the choice between a steep path straight up a hill or a gentle slope winding upward around it, most people would choose the gentler slope. Similarly, it is easier to climb a set of stairs than a vertical ladder. We do not think of such

There is very little friction between a skater's skates and the ice. That is because the pressure on the skates (because of the skater's weight) melts the ice slightly and provides a film of lubricating water.

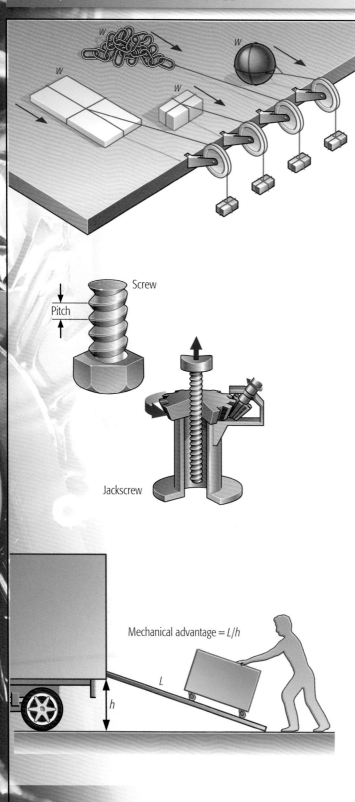

Static Friction

Static friction—the force needed to start an object sliding along a surface—depends on the object's weight, not on its shape or the area of contact between the object and the surface. All the objects shown here have the same weight (W), and static friction is the same for all of them. Lubricants reduce friction by introducing a layer of softer substance between the object and the surface.

Screws and Jacks

The mechanical advantage of a screw depends on its pitch, the distance between its threads. Rotating a screw enables it to lift things. This is the principle of the jackscrew, as used for lifting an automobile to change a tire.

Inclined Plane

It is easier to push a load up an inclined plane than to lift it up vertically. The mechanical advantage equals the length of the ramp (L) divided by its height (h).

simple devices as machines, but they are to a physicist. They are examples of an inclined plane.

We have seen that a successful machine provides a mechanical advantage greater than 1. For an inclined plane the mechanical advantage is the load (a downward force) divided by the effort (the force pushing the load up the slope), which is equal to the length of the plane divided by the height of the slope.

A wedge is a simple application of the inclined plane. Imagine driving a wedge under the edge of a heavy block. As the wedge moves in, it gradually lifts the block. This is just like pushing a block up an inclined plane, and the mechanical advantage is equal to the length of the wedge divided by its maximum thickness. Wedges have many uses, from

Each stone block used to build the Great Pyramids weighed between 2.5 and 15 tons, or as much as 30,000 pounds.

splitting logs and rocks to forming the cutting part of an ax or chisel. All other cutting tools, from saws to sandpaper, make use of the action of wedges.

It is thought that the ancient Egyptians built huge earth ramps—inclined planes—spiraling around the pyramids while they were building them. Workers hauled large blocks of stone weighing many tons up the ramps, probably on rollers to reduce friction between the blocks and the ramp. When the pyramid was finished, after many years of back-breaking work, the ramps were finally dismantled and the earth taken away to reveal the completed structure.

The wedge-shaped head of an ax efficiently cuts through wooden logs.

Mountain roads wind gradually around the mountains at a gentle angle.

WEDGES AND SCREWS

Winding a wedge (an inclined plane) around a cylinder can create much smaller spiral ramps. The result is a screw thread. When a screw is rotated in a block of wood, its threads cut into the wood and draw in the screw. Screws are tapered, but parallel-sided bolts work in the same way. The long narrow wedge that forms the thread makes a large mechanical advantage. Its value depends on the pitch of the screw, which is the distance it travels forward in one compete rotation. This, in turn, is equal to the distance between the screw's threads.

FRICTION PROS AND CONS

A screw remains in a piece of wood because of friction. Friction is a force that tends to prevent stationary objects in contact from moving. Without it a screw would unscrew itself. But in the moving parts of machines friction is a nuisance, representing a waste of energy—for example, it soaks up about half the power of an automobile engine. Oil, grease, and other lubricants between the moving parts reduce friction.

CHAPTER TWELVE

LIFTING AND MOVING WITH PULLEYS AND GEARS

Lifting heavy loads was a problem for ancient peoples, whose only help was the inclined plane and, later, the jackscrew. The problem was solved with the invention of pulleys. Later, gears were used to control the output of rotating machinery.

Most people today think of a machine as a useful device with wheels, gears, and other rotating parts. In many ways this idea is correct, although some modern machines (such as an electrical transformer) have no moving parts. We have seen levers and other simple machines on the previous pages, and nearly all of them were devised to help lift a load. One of the best lifting machines is a pulley.

MECHANICAL ADVANTAGE OF PULLEYS

The simplest pulley has a rope passing over a single grooved wheel, like the type a farmer might use to haul a bale of hay up to the hayloft. In fact, a single pulley is not really a machine at all. Its mechanical advantage (the distance moved by the effort

On this winding mechanism, the smaller gears to the left turn faster than the larger gear they drive.

This close-up of a ship's pulley shows the rope passing over the grooved wheel.

divided by the distance moved by the load) is 1, so there is no real advantage at all. And it cannot be used for lifting anything heavier than the person pulling on the rope. All the single pulley does is to change the direction of a force—the downward pull on the rope lifts up the load.

But with two or more pulleys together the situation is different. Two pulleys give a mechanical advantage of 2, three pulleys give a mechanical advantage of 3, and so on. The number of pulley wheels, or more precisely the number of ropes between them, produces the mechanical advantage of multiple pulleys, usually known as a block and tackle. With three wheels,

however, the effort has to move three times as far as the load is lifted. As a result, a lot of rope has to be pulled through the pulley block to raise the load a small distance. Such pulleys came into their own in the days of sailing ships, when they were used to haul up the heavy weight of large canvas sails. They still have many uses today, especially in the large cranes that are used for lifting heavy loads on construction sites and at shipyards.

WHEELS AND GEARS

Early sources of power included water wheels and windmills. They needed a

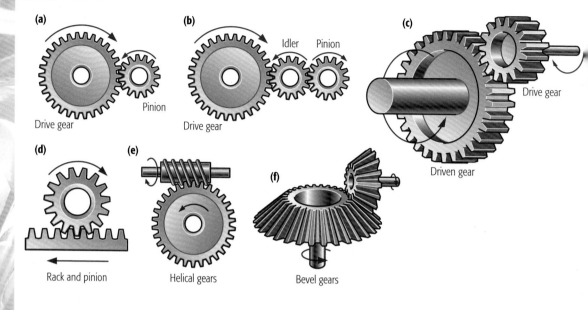

(a)

Drive gear

Pinion

(b)

Drive gear

Idler   Pinion

(c)

Drive gear

Driven gear

(d)

Rack and pinion

(e)

Helical gears

(f)

Bevel gears

DIFFERENT KINDS OF GEARS

Shown here are (a) a drive gear turning a faster pinion in the opposite direction, (b) the use of an idler gear to keep the direction of rotation the same, (c) a small drive gear turning the driven gear slower, (d) a rack and pinion, (e) a helical gear, and (f) bevel gears.

way of transferring the rotation of a shaft to other machines, such as millstones for grinding grain. One method was to link a wheel on the driven shaft to a wheel on the other machine using a rope or belt. Ropes ran on grooved wheels (like pulleys), and belts ran over wheels with flat rims. Belt drives were still in use long after the invention of the steam engine for connecting this new source of power to looms and metalworking machinery. The fan belt on a car, which enables the engine to turn the shaft of the electric generator, is a modern example of a belt drive.

By varying the sizes of the wheels—the drive wheel and the driven wheel—the speed of rotation could be changed. A large drive wheel turns a smaller driven wheel faster, whereas a small drive wheel turns a larger driven wheel slower. Both wheels rotate in the same direction, unless the belt has a half turn like a figure eight.

Larger and smaller wheels were also used when gears began to replace belt drives. Gears, also called cogwheels or cogs, are toothed wheels, usually on parallel shafts, positioned so that the teeth of one engage with the teeth of the other. Again, a large drive gear turns a smaller gear (called a pinion) faster, and a small drive gear turns a larger gear slower. The two gears rotate in opposite directions. To make the pinion gear rotate in the same direction as the drive gear, a free-running idler gear is introduced between the two.

EVEN MORE GEARS

A pinion gear driving a straight rod with teeth cut in it, called a rack, produces a side-to-side movement. It is called a rack and pinion, and is used in the steering mechanism of a car. A gear cut like a screw thread, called a helical gear, can turn another gear on a shaft at right angles to it. Another way of changing the direction of rotation through a right angle is to use bevel gears, which are cut on an angle. (See (d), (e), and (f) in the illustration to the left for these three different types.)

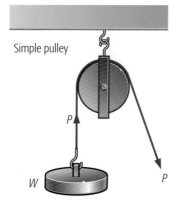

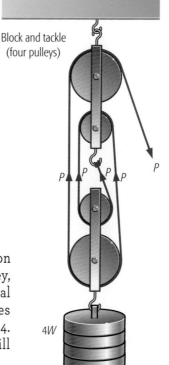

SINGLE AND MULTIPLE PULLEYS

A single pulley only changes the direction of the pull on the rope. A multiple pulley, or block and tackle, provides a mechanical advantage. With four pulleys and four ropes between them the mechanical advantage is 4. The same pull P as with the single pulley will lift a load that is four times as heavy.

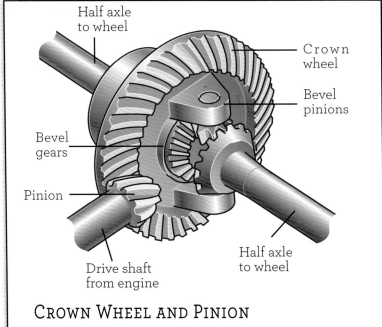

Half axle to wheel

Crown wheel

Bevel pinions

Bevel gears

Pinion

Drive shaft from engine

Half axle to wheel

CROWN WHEEL AND PINION

When a truck or car goes around a curve, the wheel on the outer side of the curve goes farther, and rotates more, than the wheel on the inside of the curve. This arrangement allows it to happen.

Tower cranes dominate the skyline at a construction site, where their main job is to lift steel girders. All the lifting movements are achieved using pulleys.

CHAPTER THIRTEEN

BIOGRAPHY: NICOLAUS COPERNICUS

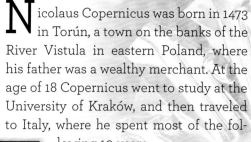

By challenging the ancient idea that the earth lay at the center of the universe, Copernicus revolutionized astronomical beliefs and has become known as the founder of modern astronomy. His theories aroused hostility among protestant church leaders.

Nicolaus Copernicus was born in 1473 in Torún, a town on the banks of the River Vistula in eastern Poland, where his father was a wealthy merchant. At the age of 18 Copernicus went to study at the University of Kraków, and then traveled to Italy, where he spent most of the following 10 years.

Italy was a very important center of learning in medieval Europe; students traveled there from all over Europe. The University of Bologna was Italy's oldest; it had been founded in the 11th century. It quickly became the most important center in Europe for the study of law and also provided teaching in medicine and philosophy. In 1222 Italy's second university was established in

The theories of Copernicus were important to the scientific revolution.

KEY DATES

1473 Born on February 19 in Torún, Poland

1483 Father dies; adopted by his uncle Lucas Watzenrode

1496–1506 Studies law, medicine, and astronomy at the universities of Bologna, Padua, and Ferrara, in Italy

c. 1510–1514 Works on manuscript in which he theorizes that the Sun is at the center of the universe

1533 Presents his theory of a Sun-centered (heliocentric) universe in a lecture to Pope Clement VII

1543 Finally publishes heliocentric theories in his book *On the Revolutions of the Celestial Spheres*

1543 Dies on May 23 at Frauenburg

Padua; others, including Ferrara in 1391, followed. Copernicus studied philosophy, mathematics, and astronomy at all three universities during his years in Italy, and also qualified as a canon lawyer (one specializing in Church law) and physician.

PTOLEMY (CLAUDIUS PTOLEMAEUS) C. 90–168 AD

Ptolemy was an astronomer and geographer who worked in Alexandria, Egypt, in the 2nd century AD. Almost nothing is known about his life, but he was the author of several great works. In his *Guide to Geography* he tried to chart the known world; he also wrote on optics in *Optica*. The art of mapmaking was one of several other subjects that he tackled.

Ptolemy's most famous work was his *Mathematical Collection*, later called *The Greatest Collection* or *Al Majisti* in Arabic. The Arabic name was corrupted to *Almagest*, and this is the name by which the work is still known. The text summarizes work carried out by ancient astronomers, and also presents new work by Ptolemy; the astronomy described in the book became known as the Ptolemaic system. In this the Earth stood at the center of the universe, surrounded by the eight crystal spheres described by Aristotle. Each sphere carried a different heavenly body—the Sun, Moon, and the five known planets; the eighth carried the stars. It was this system that Copernicus questioned.

MEASURING THE WORLD

In the days before complex measuring instruments and satellites, astronomers had to rely on simpler methods. In the 3rd century BC Greek astronomer Eratosthenes (c. 276–194 BC) worked out how big the Earth was using just a pole, or "gnomon." He knew that at Syene (now Aswan), in Egypt, no shadow was cast by a gnomon at midday on midsummer's day because the Sun was then directly overhead. When he measured the shadow cast by a gnomon at Alexandria at exactly the same time he found that the Sun's rays fell at an angle of 7o from the vertical. Once he had calculated the distance between Alexandria and Syene (about 500 miles [800 km]), he was able to compute the circumference of the Earth to within about 130 miles (209 km) of the correct figure. By Copernicus's day astronomers had a range of devices to help in their observations. The armillary sphere, a globe of the heavens, consisted of a number of calibrated metal rings representing the celestial equator, horizon, and so on. These allowed astronomers to calculate the position of the stars. The plane astrolabe had a disk with a movable chart of the heavens and a pointer for measuring angles. The quadrant, consisting of a quarter circle marked in degrees with a movable arm to measure the altitude of stars, was convenient to use. Astronomers continued to rely on them to work out the position of stars and planets even after celestial telescopes were improved in the early 17th century.

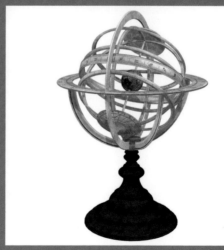

Astrolabes were used by medieval scientists to work out the position of heavenly bodies, and by sailors to help them plot their position. They had a circular disk marked in degrees and a movable pointer.

On his return to Poland in 1506, Copernicus served as secretary to his uncle Lucas, who was Bishop of Ermland, and lived at the bishop's official residence of Heilsberg Castle. After his uncle died in 1512, Copernicus moved to Frauenburg in East Prussia, where he was appointed a canon of the cathedral. A canon is one

REFORMING THE CALENDAR

In 1514 Pope Leo X (1475–1521) invited Copernicus to Rome to advise the Church on revising the calendar. The existing calendar had been established in the 1st century BC by the Roman statesman Julius Caesar (100/102– 44 BC), and was named the Julian calendar for him. The Julian calendar had replaced the old lunar calendar (one based on the phases of the Moon). In reforming the calendar, Caesar called on the help of the Alexandrian astronomer Sosigenes, and it was Sosigenes who suggested basing the new calendar on a solar calendar (one related to the Sun), with a year length of 365¼ days. He then divided this into months based on the seasons. To achieve an average year length of 365¼ days, it was decided that three years should be 365 days long, and the fourth should be 366 days: this extra day still appears in the modern calendar every four years, called leap year, as February 29. There was a 90-day difference between the old lunar calendar and the new Julian one, which came into use in 46 BC. To make up this gap, officials inserted 23 extra days after February 23 and 67 extra days at the end of November. That year was 445 days long.

The new calendar seemed to be much more accurate; the fact that each year was just over 11 minutes too long did not seem to matter. However, as the years went by the seasons again became increasingly out of phase with the calendar, leading to the pope's invitation to Copernicus to revise it. He turned it down, arguing that it was important to work out the proper motions of the solar system before attempting any revisions. By 1545 the spring equinox, used to calculate the date of Easter, was 10 days adrift from the calendar date.

It was not until 1582 that attempts were again made to revise the calendar: Pope Gregory XIII (1502–1585) adjusted it by jumping straight from October 5 to 15. Now the length of the year was accepted as 365.2422 days, which differed from the Julian calendar by 3.12 days every 400 years. Leap years were still retained every four years. But to make sure the calendar stayed in phase with the solar year it was decided that centennial years (those divisible by 100 as well as by 4) should not be kept as leap years. The only exceptions were quatercentennial years (those divisible by 400). That is why the year 2000 was a leap year but 1700, 1800, and 1900 were not.

The new calendar, known as the Gregorian, was adopted throughout Catholic Europe in 1582. Britain and America did not begin using it until 1752. Other countries were slower still; the Soviet Union adopted it only in 1918 and Greece in 1923.

POPE GREGORY XIII

Ptolemy, seen here in a portrait dating to the medieval period, was a Roman citizen. He wrote in the Greek language and lived in Alexandria, Egypt, which was a province of Rome.

of the priests responsible for organizing cathedral services and looking after the building. It was not a very demanding post, and it allowed him ample time to pursue his study of astronomy.

ARISTOTLE'S VIEW

The Greek philosopher Aristotle had described his view of the universe in the 4th century BC, in which transparent spheres carried heavenly bodies in perfectly circular orbits around an immobile Earth. However, astronomers watching the heavenly bodies could see that the Sun, the Moon, and the planets did not actually move in this way. To allow for this, the astronomer Ptolemy (c. 90–168 AD) had to introduce a number of complications into the system. One of his proposals was that while the Earth remained at the center of a planet's orbit, the planet moved in another cycle, called an epicycle, centered on its own orbit, or "deferent." This was the only way Ptolemy could justify Aristotle's view that the heavenly bodies moved at uniform speeds throughout their orbits. More than 1,000 years later this system, called the Ptolemaic system, was still accepted as essentially correct.

A MOVING SUN

There appeared to be good reason for taking Ptolemy's view of the universe as true. Firstly, the Sun does seem to move across the sky each day, rising in the east, climbing and descending in a slow arc, and finally setting in the west. To an observer the Sun, rather than the Earth, appears to be moving. Secondly, astronomers reasoned that the Earth could not rotate on its own axis (a view held by some ancient Greek philosophers, including Philolaos [c. 530 BC]) because if it did, why didn't buildings collapse or people feel a tremendous rush of wind against their faces? Why did an apple falling from a tree land at the tree's foot and not behind it? In the time it took the apple to fall to the ground, wouldn't the Earth have moved around some distance, taking the tree with it?

A third argument in favor of the idea that the Earth was stationary and the Sun moved was based on a famous passage in the Bible. The prophet Joshua had commanded: "Sun, stand thou still..." (Joshua 10:12–14), and to Christian thinkers in the Middle Ages this suggested that the Sun moved at God's will.

HELIOSTATIC UNIVERSE

Copernicus was the first astronomer since the time of the Greeks to challenge these views. He identified a number of problems with the Ptolemaic system, in particular Ptolemy's belief

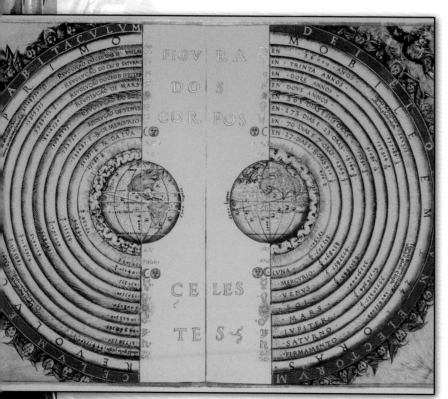

This 1568 illustration by Bartolomeu Velho shows a model of a geocentric universe, in which the Sun and planets move around a stationary Earth.

GEORG JOACHIM VON LAUCHEN (KNOWN AS RHETICUS) 1514–1574

Rheticus was born in 1514 in Feldkirch, Austria. In 1536 he was appointed professor of mathematics and astronomy at Wittenberg. There he heard of Copernicus's theory of a Sun-centered universe and, fascinated by the idea, traveled to Poland to visit and study with Copernicus. After persuading Copernicus to publish his theory, Rheticus later produced his own great work, *The Palatine Work on Triangles*, which was completed after his death by his pupil Valentin Otto and finally published in 1596. The book contains trigonometric tables to calculate arcs and angles.

that the planets moved in one circle around the equant while maintaining a uniform speed in another circle around the earth. Copernicus thought that this was altogether too complicated. He was in favor of a simpler system, in which bodies moved in a uniform circular motion around a single point. Consequently, in about 1510, he began to explore other possibilities that would fit the available evidence.

Copernicus now began to share the view of Aristarchus of Samos and some other Greek thinkers that the Earth circles the Sun rather than the other way around. In other words, he thought that the universe is "heliostatic" (the word is from the Greek and means "stationary Sun"). In his book, *On the Revolutions of the Celestial Spheres* (which was not published until the year he died, 1543), Copernicus pointed out that, whether it is the Earth or the heavens that are moving, the results will seem the same to an observer. We could be situated on an Earth that is standing still while the stars revolve around us, or on an Earth that performs a complete orbit every 24 hours; in both cases, the stars would appear to revolve around us. We have all been on a moving ship or in a traveling car that we think is standing still. We believe

This modern illustration shows the Earth and other planets moving in orbit around the Sun.

If the people in a moving car look outside, their view is the same whether they are moving forward or the other cars are moving backward.

that the other ships or vehicle we see are moving when in fact they are stationary. So, Copernicus argued, it is with the Earth and the stars and Sun. Copernicus decided that all the planets, including the Earth, moved around the Sun, and that the Moon revolved around the Earth. Copernicus believed that this would explain much more simply why the other planets moved in the way they did, and why there was a variation in the brightness of the planets. Copernicus was even able to place the planets in order from the Sun: Mercury was nearest, then Venus, then Earth, Mars, Jupiter, and Saturn (the other planets were still undiscovered at this date). Copernicus also took up the idea first argued by some earlier Greek astronomers that the Earth spins, or rotates, daily on its axis.

Copernicus believed that this arrangement fit more accurately with how the planets appeared to move, and it was more simple than the Ptolemaic system. However, Copernicus continued to accept the Aristotelian idea that there were eight transparent spheres carrying the five known planets, the Sun, the Moon, and the stars, and that the planets moved in perfect circular motion.

GOING AGAINST THE CHURCH

Copernicus completed *On the Revolutions of the Celestial Spheres* in 1514, but did not publish it until 1543.

The reason for this delay is not clear. It is possible that he might have been concerned about the reaction of the Church. At this time in Europe the Catholic Church was still extremely powerful; in 1551 the pope, the leader of the Catholic Church in Rome, declared that people should not just follow reason but should confirm "their opinions with the Holy Scripture, Traditions of the Apostles, sacred and approved Councils, and by the Constitutions and Authorities of the holy Fathers." By this he meant that people should make sure that their opinions were in line with those of the Catholic Church. So there did appear to be some

risks for Copernicus if he published his theory because it contradicted a biblical text and suggested that humankind, which was supposed to have been created in God's image, did not stand at the very center of the universe. Many years later, in 1633, the Italian astronomer named Galileo Galilei (1564–1642) would experience the full force of the Church's anger when he was put on trial for supporting Copernicus's theory.

However, nearly a century before Galileo's trial it was the Protestant reformer Martin Luther (1483–1546) who seemed most horrified by Copernicus's new theories. Luther was leader of the

This painting by the 19th-century Polish artist Jan Mateijko shows Copernicus, surrounded by astronomical instruments, in his roofless observatory. He built it on the fortified walls of Frauenburg Cathedral, which can be seen in the background.

attack on corruption in the Roman Catholic Church that resulted in the movement known as the Reformation. The Reformation led to a break with the pope and the establishment of the Protestant faith. Pointing out that "sacred Scripture tells us that Joshua commanded the Sun to stand still, and not the Earth," Luther dismissed Copernicus in no uncertain terms as an upstart astrologer and a fool. His fellow reformer Philipp Melanchthon (1497–1560) added to Luther's objections by commenting that, "...It is want of honesty and decency to assert such notions publicly, and the example is pernicious."

FOR MATHEMATICIANS ONLY

Copernicus had already presented his theory of a Sun-centered universe in a lecture to Pope Clement VII in 1533, so in fact his reluctance to publish his ideas seems to have had more to do with his concerns about people misunderstanding his arguments than with threats from the Church. Copernicus claimed that he had deliberately made his work as technical as possible so that it could be judged only by mathematicians, insisting that, "Mathematics is for mathematicians." He also added to the title page of his book the motto taken from Plato's Academy: "let no one enter who knows no Geometry."

One of Martin Luther's major disagreements with the Catholic Church was whether forgiveness from God's punishment could be purchased through indulgences.

In 1633 Galileo, seen here, was tried by the Church and found guilty of heresy for supporting the theories of Copernicus. He spent the rest of this life under house arrest.

CHOOSING TO PUBLISH

Copernicus might never have published *On the Revolutions of the Celestial Spheres* had it not been for the young Georg Joachim von Lauchen (1514–1574), an Austrian-born scholar who is better known by the latin name of Rheticus. Rheticus had learned of Copernicus's theory of a Sun-centered universe in Wittenberg, Germany, where he was professor of mathematics. Coincidentally, Wittenberg was also where Martin Luther was a professor. The Protestant Reformation had begun in Wittenberg when Luther pinned to the church door there articles—known as the Ninety-Five Theses—that were highly critical of the pope and the clergy.

In 1539, aged only 25, Rheticus arrived unannounced at Copernicus's home. He stayed there for nearly two years. It was a surprising alliance that developed between the two: Rheticus was an energetic and ambitious young man, and Copernicus was an aging and retiring priest. In addition, Rheticus was a Protestant visiting a Catholic at a time in the early Reformation when religious differences could cost a man his job, his freedom, and even his life.

Johannes Gutenberg was the inventor of the moveable type printing press.

PRINTING WITH A PREFACE

Printing had been invented in Mainz, Germany, about a century earlier. Known popularly as the German art, it spread rapidly to all the major centers of commerce and learning. By about 1470 Nuremberg, in southern Germany, had became the chief center of a flourishing book publishing industry. It was here that Copernicus's text was taken for publication. Unknown to Copernicus, an addition was made to his text by the priest Andreas Osiander (1498–1522). Osiander was a supporter of Luther, and he had been shown the text by Rheticus. Osiander inserted a preface saying that Copernicus's theory was only a way of tying in calculations with observations, and that it should not be taken literally. This disclaimer might have made the work more acceptable to the public. By the time it was ready for publication Copernicus had suffered a stroke. A first copy of the printed book is said to have been brought to him at Frauenberg on the day he died.

During this time Rheticus set about mastering the Copernican system of the universe, and in 1540 he published a brief description of it in *First Account of the Book On the Revolutions by Nicolaus Copernicus*. Eventually Rheticus managed to persuade Copernicus to have his manuscript printed, and to allow it to be circulated to a wider public.

CRITICISMS AND PROOF

Copernicus's ideas were now revealed to other astronomers, the Church, and the public. The most important astronomical criticism came from the Danish astronomer Tycho Brahe (1546–1601). Brahe argued that if the Earth were orbiting the Sun once a year as Copernicus claimed, then anyone observing the stars on a regular basis would view them from widely different observational points during the course of the year, and so should expect to see a shift in the pattern of the stars. Because astronomers of the time could not see any such shift, they decided that the Earth could not be moving. In fact, the shift does take place. It is called annual parallax. It is similar to the effect that can be achieved if you close one eye and focus on a distant object; if you then open that eye and close the other one, you will notice that the object shifts slightly.

Copernicus had already considered this point. He was convinced that the parallax could not be seen because the stars were so far away. This was another point of dispute; many astronomers of the time could not imagine that God would design a universe in which such a huge space stood between the stars and the planets. Copernicus was correct, though. There is annual parallax, but it was not detected until 1838 when the German astronomer Friedrich Bessel (1784–1846), was able to detect a slight degree of parallax in the star 61 Cygni, about 10.3 light-years from earth (the nearest known star, Proxima Centauri, is about 4.26 light-years away).

This 1566 printing of Copernicus' work is printed in Latin.

Copernicus was buried in Frombork Cathedral, in Poland. In 2005 his remains were discovered by a team of archaeologists. In 2010 Copernicus was reburied and the spot is now identified with a granite tombstone.

SCIENTIFIC BACKGROUND

Before 1480

Greek philosopher Aristarchus of Samos (c. 310–230 BC) teaches that the Earth orbits a stationary Sun, but his theory is not widely accepted

Astronomer Ptolemy of Alexandria (c. 90–168 AD) sums up Greek astronomy, principally that the Earth is at the center of the cosmos

1483 The *Alfonsine Tables*, a revision of the *Ptolemaic Tables* of planetary positions, are printed in Toledo, Spain

1497 Copernicus observes and records the temporary disappearance of a star behind the Moon

1504 Columbus frightens a group of Native Americans by correctly predicting a total eclipse of the Moon on February 29

1514 Copernicus writes the first version of his heliocentric (Sun-centered) theory, but does not publish it for nearly 30 years

1540 The Austrian-born mathematician and astronomer Rheticus (1514–74) publishes his *First Account* of Copernicus's heliocentric theory

1543 Copernicus publishes his heliocentric theory in *On the Revolutions of the Celestial Spheres*

After 1550

1577 Danish astronomer Tycho Brahe (1546–1601) shows that comets move in spaces between planets, and do not lie within the Earth's atmosphere

1609 German astronomer Johannes Kepler (1571–1630) shows that planetary motion is elliptical, and that the speed of a planet's orbit speeds up when it is nearer the Sun and slows down when it is farther away

1616 Copernicus's book is placed on the Catholic *Index of Prohibited Books*

POLITICAL AND CULTURAL BACKGROUND

1474 English printer William Caxton (c. 1422– c. 1491) prints the first ever book in the English language, *Recuyell of the Historyes of Troye*

c. 1484 The High Renaissance blooms in Italy; Italian artist Sandro Botticelli (1444–1510) paints his mythological work, *The Birth of Venus*

1492 In a period of great exploration, Genoese sailor Christopher Columbus (1451–1506) becomes the first European to discover the New World

1497 Genoese-born Venetian explorer John Cabot (Giovanni Caboto, 1425–c. 1500) sights North America, claiming the land for England

c. 1504 Italian painter Leonardo da Vinci (1452–1519) completes his most famous picture, the *Mona Lisa*

1508–12 Italian painter and sculptor Michelangelo (1475–1564) paints the Sistine Chapel ceiling in Rome

1517 German religious reformer Martin Luther (1483–1546) instigates the Protestant Reformation by displaying articles critical of the Catholic Church on the castle church door at Wittenberg

1519 Spanish conquistador Hernando Cortés (1485–1547) begins his conquest of the Aztec empire in Mexico on behalf of Spain

1526 The Mogul dynasty of Muslim emperors is established in India; Moguls will rule there for more than 330 years

1533 Aged three, Ivan IV (1530–84) assumes power of Russia; his savage rule earns him the name "Ivan the Terrible"

1534 English King Henry VIII (1491–1547), who wants to divorce his first wife and remarry, breaks with Roman Catholic Rome and heads a newly established Church of England

1545–63 The Council of Trent attempts to define doctrine and reform abuses in the Roman Catholic Church; it marks the start of a Counter-Reformation against Protestants

acceleration The rate of change in a moving object's velocity. It is a vector quantity.

acceleration due to gravity Also called acceleration of free fall, the acceleration of any object with mass falling freely under the Earth's gravity. Its symbol is g.

air resistance A force, also called drag or wind resistance, that resists the movement of an object through the air. It is overcome by streamlining.

ampere (A) The SI unit of electric current.

balance A device for finding an object's mass by comparing it with known masses. Devices for finding an object's weight, perhaps by noting how much it stretches a vertical spring, are also called balances. See also *equilibrium*.

block and tackle A multiple pulley, one with two or more pulley wheels.

candela (cd) The SI unit of luminous intensity.

center of gravity Also called center of mass, the point at which an object's total mass appears to be concentrated and at which it acts.

center of mass Another name for center of gravity.

centrifugal force A fictitious force sometimes said to act in opposition to (and therefore to balance) the centripetal force.

centripetal force The force that acts inward to keep an object moving in a circle.

classes of lever See *lever*.

conservation of energy Energy can be neither created nor destroyed, just changed from one form to another.

conservation of momentum In a collision the total momentum of the objects after impact is the same as it was before impact.

couple The effect of two moments acting on an object in the same sense (i.e. both clockwise or both counterclockwise) at the same time.

effort In a simple machine the input force (such as that applied to move a load).

energy The capacity to do work. There are various kinds, including kinetic energy, potential energy, and strain energy. Heat, light, and sound are also forms of energy. Energy is measured in joules.

equilibrium A state of physical balance. If an object in stable equilibrium is tilted, its center of gravity rises, and when released, it falls back to its original position. If an object in neutral equilibrium is tilted, its center of gravity neither rises nor falls, and the object merely rolls. If an object in unstable equilibrium is tilted, its center of gravity falls, and the object topples over.

fluid A gas or a liquid.

force An influence that changes the shape, position, or movement of an object.

force of gravity Also called gravitation, the force between any two objects arising from their masses, most often applied to the force between an object and the Earth (the object's weight).

force ratio Another name for mechanical advantage.

free fall The state of an object that is falling under the Earth's force of gravity.

friction A force that prevents or slows the movement of one surface against another surface.

fulcrum A pivot, as on a seesaw or where a lever pivots.

gas A state of matter in which the molecules move at random and take on the size and shape of their container.

gravitation Another name for the force of gravity.

hertz (Hz) The derived SI unit of frequency.

inclined plane A simple machine consisting of a ramp; the effort is used to push a load up the ramp. A wedge used to split things is also an inclined plane.

inertia The property of an object that makes it tend to resist being moved or, if moving, to resist a change in direction. It is a consequence of the first of Newton's laws of motion.

joule (J) The derived SI unit of energy equal to the amount of work done when a force of 1 newton acts through a distance of 1 meter.

kelvin (K) The SI unit of thermodynamic temperature.

kilogram (kg) The SI unit of mass, equal to 1,000 grams.

kinetic energy The energy an object possesses because it is moving.

laws of motion See *Newton's laws of motion*.

lever A simple machine. There are three types or classes: In a Class 1 lever the load and effort are on opposite sides of the fulcrum and act in the same direction. In a Class 2 lever the load and effort are on the same side of the fulcrum but act in opposite directions; the load is nearer the fulcrum than is the effort. In a Class 3 lever the load and effort are on the same side of the fulcrum and act in the opposite direction; the effort is nearer the fulcrum than is the load.

liquid A state of matter, between a gas and a solid, that has a level surface and, below that surface, takes on the shape of its container.

load In a simple machine the output force (such as that applied by the effort).

luminous intensity The light-emitting power of a source of light.

machine A device that allows one force (the effort) to overcome another (the load).

mass The amount of matter in an object. See also *weight*.

mechanical advantage Also called force ratio, in a simple machine it is the load divided by the effort.

meter (m) The SI unit of length.

metric system The system of weights and measures, based originally on the meter, from which the system of SI units was developed.

mole (mol) The SI unit for quantity of matter.

moment The turning effect (torque) produced when a force acts on an object, equal to the force multiplied by the perpendicular distance of its line of action to the pivot.

momentum The mass of an object multiplied by its velocity in a straight line.

newton (N) The derived SI unit of force. It is the force required to give a mass of 1 kilogram an acceleration of 1 meter per second per second.

Newton's laws of motion Three laws about moving objects: 1. An object at rest will stay at rest, or a moving object will go on moving, unless a force acts on it. 2. The force acting on a moving object is equal to its mass multiplied by its acceleration. 3. When one object exerts a force on another (the action), the second object exerts the same force but in the opposite direction (the reaction). In other words, action and reaction are equal and opposite.

potential energy The energy an object possesses because of its position (such as a weight that has been raised to a certain height above the ground).

power The rate of doing work or the rate at

which energy changes. It is measured in watts.

pulley A simple machine consisting of a fixed grooved wheel with a rope running around it. A mechanical advantage of more than 1 can be achieved only by using two or more pulleys together.

scalar A quantity that has magnitude but (unlike a vector) no specified direction. Examples of scalars are speed and mass.

second (s) The SI unit of time. (The second is also an angular measure, equal to 1/60 of a minute or 1/3,600 of a degree.)

SI units The system of units used internationally in science (short for Système International d'Unités, its name in French). There are seven base units (ampere, candela, kelvin, kilogram, meter, mole, and second) and various derived units, which are combinations of base units.

speed A moving object's rate of change of position (distance traveled divided by time taken). It is a scalar quantity (unlike velocity, which is a vector).

standard form A way of expressing very large or very small numbers that uses an index to represent powers of 10. For example, 10,000,000 is 10^7 and 0.000002 is 2×10^{-6}.

strain energy The energy an object possesses because its structure is strained (such as a stretched rubber band).

streamlining The shaping of an object so that it presents the least resistance when moving through a fluid (gas or liquid).

terminal speed The maximum speed at which an object falls under the influence of gravity.

torque The turning effect of a force on an object. See *moment*.

triangle of forces A way of adding forces using the triangle of vectors.

triangle of vectors A way of adding vectors. The first vector is drawn as a line at the correct angle, with the length of the line representing its magnitude. The second vector is drawn from the end of the first line, again at the correct angle and of the correct length. A third line joining the beginning of the first line to the end of the second line (completing the triangle) gives the magnitude and direction of the sum of the vectors.

vector A quantity that has magnitude and (unlike a scalar) direction. Examples of vectors include acceleration and velocity.

velocity A moving object's rate of change of position in a specified direction (distance traveled divided by the time taken). It is a vector quantity (unlike speed, which is a scalar).

watt (W) The derived SI unit of power (equal to a rate of working of 1 joule per second).

weight The force with which a mass is attracted toward the Earth (by the force of gravity).

wheel and axle A simple machine in which a rope is attached to the rim of a wheel, which is fixed to an axle that has another rope wrapped around it. Pulling on the rope to turn the wheel (applying an effort) turns the axle so that its rope will lift a load.

work The energy used when a force moves an object or changes its shape. It is measured in joules.

Copernicus Science Centre
Wybrzeże Kościuszkowskie 20
00-390 Warsaw, Poland
+48 (0) 22 596 41 10
Web site: http://www.kopernik.org.pl/en/
This science museum is the largest of its
   kind in Poland and one of the most
   advanced in Europe. It contains over
   450 interactive exhibits that allow
   visitors to perform experiments and
   discover the laws of science
   first-hand!

Hoover Dam
NV SR 172
Nevada-Arizona border
702-494-2517
Web site: https://www.usbr.gov/lc/
   hooverdam/index.html
The Hoover Dam stretches across the
   Colorado River, and is an excellent
   opportunity to see both potential
   and kinetic energy in action. Hoover
   Dam generates about 4 billion kilo-
   watt-hours of hydroelectric power
   each year, or enough to serve 1.3 million people in the states of Nevada,
   Arizona, and California.

Kennedy Space Center
State Road 405
Cape Canaveral, FL, 32899
312-867-5000
Web site: http://www.kennedyspacecen-
   ter.com/
Kennedy Space Center has been the
   launch site of manned US space
   shuttles since 1968. A visit to the
space center includes the US
Astronaut Hall of Fame, IMAX films,
exhibits on the history of human
space exploration, and a close-up
experience with the space shuttle
Atlantis.

National Atomic Testing Museum
755 E. Flamingo Rd.
Las Vegas, NV 89119
702-794-5151
Web site: http://www.nationalatomictest-
   ingmuseum.org/
This museum, part of the Smithsonian
   Institute, traces the conception,
   development, and testing of the
   atomic bomb. Exhibits on such top-
   ics as radiation and underground
   testing are on permanent display.

National Institute of Standards and
   Technology
100 Bureau Drive
Stop 1070
Gaithersburg, MD 20899
301-975-6478
Web site: http://www.nist.gov/
The National Institute of Standards and
   Technology, or NIST, is a federal
   agency within the US Department of
   Commerce. Its mission is to "pro-
   mote US innovation and industrial
   competitiveness by advancing measurement science, standards, and
   technology." The agency has a cam-
   pus in Gaithersburg, Maryland, and
   one in Boulder, Colorado.

National Museum of Mathematics
11 East 26th Street
New York, NY 10010
212-542-0566
Web site: http://momath.org/
This museum, which opened in 2012,
seeks to spark visitors' curiosity and
illuminate the wonder of mathematics in the world. Visitors can
experience hands-on exhibits, such
as Math Midway, and take advantage
of a lecture series called Math
Encounters.

Physical Measurements Laboratory
100 Bureau Drive
Stop 1070
Gaithersburg, MD 20899
301-975-6478
Web site: http://www.nist.gov/pml/
index.cfm
Part of the National Institute of
Standards and Technology, the
Physical Measurements Laboratory
sets the US standard of every measurement used in business and
research, including length, mass,
force and shock, acceleration, temperature, and many others. The
laboratory also devises procedures
and tools to progress the science of
measurement around the world.

Woolsthorpe Manor
Water Lane, Woolsthorpe by
Colsterworth, near Grantham
Lincolnshire, NG33 5PD
+44 (0) 1476860338

Web site: http://www.nationaltrust.org.
uk/woolsthorpe-manor/
This restored estate is the birthplace of
Sir Isaac Newton. The area is under
the care of the National Trust, an
organization with the aim of preserv-
ing heritage sites and open spaces.
The site includes a Science Centre
and Light Workshop, as well as the
400-year-old "Gravity Tree," a Flower
of Kent apple tree that inspired
Newton's theories on gravity.

WEB SITES

Due to the changing nature of Internet
links, Rosen Publishing has developed
an online list of Web sites related to the
subject of this book. This site is updated
regularly. Please use this link to access
the list:

http://www.rosenlinks.com/CORE/Mech

Aristotle, David Bostock, and Robin Waterfield. *Physics*. Oxford World Classics. Oxford, UK: Oxford University Press, 2008.

Clegg, Brian. *Gravity: How the Weakest Force in the Universe Shaped Our Lives*. New York: St. Martin's Press, 2012.

Darling, David. *Gravity's Arc: The Story of Gravity from Aristotle to Einstein and Beyond*. Hoboken, NJ: Wiley Publishers, 2006.

Dolnick, Edward. *The Clockwork Universe: Isaac Newton, the Royal Society, and the Birth of the Modern World*. New York: Harper Perennial, 2012.

Fox, Michael H. *Why We Need Nuclear Power: The Environmental Case*. Oxford, UK: Oxford University Press, 2014.

Galilei, Galileo, and Maurice A. Finocchiaro. *The Essential Galileo*. Cambridge, MA: Hackett Publishing Company, 2009.

Gingerich, Owen. *The Book Nobody Read: Chasing the Revolutions of Nicolaus Copernicus*. New York: Walker Books, 2009.

Glover, David. *Pulleys and Gears*. Simple Machines. Chicago: Heinemann Library, 2006.

Glover, David. *Ramps and Wedges*. Simple Machines. Chicago: Heinemann Library, 2006.

Koscielniak, Bruce. *About Time: A First Look at Time and Clocks*. New York: HMH Books for Young Readers, 2014.

Macy, Christine. *Dams*. Library of Congress Visual Sourcebooks. New York: W. W. Norton and Company, 2009.

Newton, Isaac, and Dana Densmore. *Selections from Newton's Principia*. Santa Fe, NM: Green Lion Press, 2005.

Seeds, Michael A., and Dana Backman. *Horizons: Exploring the Universe*. Independence, KY: Cengage Learning, 2013.

Silverman, Buffy. *Simple Machines*. Forces in Action. Chicago: Heinemann Library, 2009.

Sobel, Dava. *A More Perfect Heaven: How Copernicus Revolutionized the Cosmos*. New York: Walker and Company, 2013.

Wootton, David. *Galileo: Watcher of the Skies*. New Haven, CT: Yale University Press, 2014.

Yasuda, Anita. *Explore Simple Machines!: With 25 Great Projects*. Explore Your World. White River Junction, VT: Nomad Press, 2012.

Zimba, Jason. *Force and Motion: An Illustrated Guide to Newton's Laws*. Baltimore, MD: Johns Hopkins University Press, 2009.

PHOTO CREDITS